The Enthusiast's Book of
GARDENING LATIN

Michael Streeter

First published in Great Britain in 2003 by

Past Times, Oxford, England

© 2003 Complete Editions

Designed by seagulls

Manufactured in Thailand by Imago

PAST TIMES®

Contents

Latin and Plants
– An Introduction

Many gardeners are baffled by the Latin names of plants. The words can be long, hard to pronounce and – worst of all – apparently meaningless.

Help, however, is at hand. *The Enthusiast's Book of Gardening Latin* will help you unlock the secrets of the language used to describe plants. In the course of these pages, we will discover the hidden meanings of the names, learn what those names tell us about a plant and in the process help us become better gardeners. The bewildering barrage of words will no longer be an obstacle between ourselves and the plants we love. Indeed, we will discover why Latin – a famously dead language – is such a useful ally in understanding that most alive of subjects – the plant kingdom.

Why Latin?

The reason we use Latin in gardening is simply because of history. Until the nineteenth century, Latin was the universal language of science. Though it had not been spoken by ordinary folk for hundreds of years, the language clung on to one crucial role – enabling scientists and academics from different countries to understand one another.

To take just one example, Sir Isaac Newton's greatest work, entitled *Principia Mathematica* and published in 1687, was written in Latin, ensuring it was intelligible to all people of learning in the seventeenth century.

Though English has now assumed the mantle of global language for science and technology, Latin still plays a major role in the classification of the natural world. This is especially true with plants, and the reason for this is simple. When plants were first put into a formal classification in the eighteenth century, Latin was still the international language of science. The man behind this classification was called Carl Linnaeus.

Carl Linnaeus

Linnaeus was a Swedish scientist born in 1707. A medical doctor by training, his great passion was botany and he devised a new way of classifying plants. This classification was long overdue, because before Linnaeus's work the naming of plants had been haphazard and confusing. As more and more plants were discovered and identified, gardeners and botanists could not simply continue using common names for plants or inventing long rambling descriptions in Latin. The main problem with using everyday names, for example, was that these differ not just from country to country but from region to region. Consider the plane tree; a plane tree means one thing in England, another in Scotland – and something different again in the United States. And who is to know that 'Love-in-idleness', 'Heartsease', 'Wild pansy' and 'Johnny-jump-up' are all names referring to the plant that is known botanically as *Viola tricolor*?

The work of Linnaeus helped to bring order to this chaos. He developed what is called the 'binomial' system – the word binomial simply meaning 'two names' – and he developed it in Latin.

A Divided Kingdom

The plant kingdom is divided by scientists into many different categories. These are division, class, order, family, genus and species.

But the two that really matter to the everyday gardener are the last two, the *genus* (plural *genera*) and the *species*. It is these two categories that form Linnaeus's binomial method of naming. In this system, each plant has two Latin names: one is the name of the genus it belongs to – its generic name; the other is the name of its species – its specific name.

A *genus* is a group of different plant species which share certain characteristics. The genus name may tell you something about the plant, it may simply be invented or may be the name by which those plants have been known for hundreds of years – though now in Latinized form.

Within a genus there may be a few or hundreds of *species*. A species refers to a group of individual plants with common characteristics which make them different from others, and which can breed among themselves. The species name often tells you something about the plant, for example its size, the colour of its flowers, where it likes to grow or where it originates. Sometimes it tells you who first identified it. In the next section, we will uncover the various meanings of these Latin names.

Naming a Plant

For now, let us return to the example of the 'Wild pansy' we mentioned earlier to see how this naming system works in practice. Its botanical name is *Viola tricolor*. The first word, *Viola*, tells you the plant is from the genus *Viola*. The second word tells you that its specific, identifying name is *tricolor*. This name means three-coloured. The name *Viola tricolor* is unique to this plant. There may be (and indeed are) many other plants called '*Viola something*'. There may be (and are) other plants called '*Something tricolor*'. But there is only one species of plant called *Viola tricolor*. Which means that whether you live in Timbuktu, Telford or Tallahassee, if you come across this plant's name, you know which plant is being talked about. Note also that the genus name always comes first, followed by the species name.

Cultivars

This system of naming works for all plant species. However, there are varieties in form and shape of plants which – while not botanically significant – are vital for the gardener. Variations in the colour and shape of the flowers are obvious examples. These varieties can occur naturally, but they are also encouraged in cultivation by gardeners and professional growers. These are known as cultivated varieties – or 'cultivars' for short. For the gardener, these cultivars must have names too, to distinguish plants from similar plants of the same species.

This is done by adding an additional name to the species name of the plant. This name does not necessarily describe the plant, it is simply its cultivar name. Often it is named after a person. Our example *Viola tricolor*, for example, has a cultivar called *Viola tricolor* 'Bowles' Black'.

Usually both the genus and the species name are written *before* the cultivar name, as in the example just given. Sometimes when the species name is uncertain, perhaps because of cross-breeding, the cultivar name is given after just the genus name. In this case it would be written *Viola* 'Bowles' Black'. Occasionally we see other variations in plants names. For example an 'x' sometimes appears between the genus name and the species name, as in *Ilex* x *meserveae* (blue holly). This shows that this is a hybrid or 'cross' between two different species of the holly genus *Ilex*. More rarely the cross comes *before* the genus name, as in x *Cupressocyparis leylandii* (Leyland cypress). This means it is a cross between two species of different genera.

Finally, where there are separate names for natural variations, different forms or subspecies of plants, these are indicated respectively as: 'var.', 'f.' and 'subsp.'. For example, one subspecies of snowdrop is known as *Galanthus plicatus* subsp. *byzantinus*.

The Correct Style

Note that the genus and species names are always written in *italics*, or if this is not possible then underlined. Also, the genus always begins with a capital letter, while the species name is lower case, as in *Viola tricolor*. If we are writing about lots of species or varieties of the same genus, then the first name can be shortened to a single letter, as in *Viola tricolor* and *V. odorata* – the Sweet pansy.

By contrast, the cultivar name is never written in italics and is put inside single inverted commas, as in *V. tricolor* 'Bowles' Black'. Nowadays, and to avoid confusion, the cultivar name is not supposed to be a Latin word, though examples of this practice from old varieties still exist.

Indeed, the need to avoid confusion in the naming of new plant species and varieties is regarded as so important that there are strict world-wide rules which govern them – known as the International Code of Botanical Nomenclature and the International Code for the Nomenclature of Cultivated Plants.

Incidentally, though the genus and species names are always in Latin *form*, many of the words may have originated in other languages. Words from Greek, English and other languages have been 'Latinized' over the years to conform to the established format.

This book generally gives the standard *–us* ending of Latin words but remember that because of grammatical rules species names can vary in their endings, often finishing with *–a* rather than *–us*. So for example we find *Penstemon grandiflorus* (the last word meaning free-flowering or large-flowered) but *Magnolia grandi-flora*. This does not however affect the meaning.

Making Sense of the Names

The key question now is how to make sense of the Latin names, once we have seen how they are put together. This is where *The Enthusiast's Book of Gardening Latin* is designed to help. In the next section we will see nearly 900 examples of Latin words used in the naming of plants – together with their meaning. We will also see how many of the longer names are combinations of shorter, easy-to-understand Latin words. From these, gardeners can learn how to spot the meanings of many other unfamiliar plant names with little or no effort.

In the final section there are eighty common plant names. Alongside are their botanical names, some details on how they got those names and the names of closely-related plants.

Together, these two sections will take the anxiety out of browsing plant catalogues, and the fear out of long Latin names at the garden centre. Once the secrets to the naming of plants are known, we no longer need to be confused by the apparently obscure language which describes them.

What Latin Names Mean

Prefixes

A number of Latin names for plant species are effectively made up of two words. These two parts are the main word, plus a 'prefix' added to the front of it, which alters its meaning. Take the Latin word for purple, *purpureus* or *purpurea*. If we add the prefix *atro-* which means dark, then we get *atropurpureus*, which means 'dark purple'. By getting to know some of the more common prefixes, which are listed in the following pages, we can begin to understand the meaning of words that are quite unfamiliar to us. For example, if we see a plant which begins with *calli-* then we will know that at least part of that plant is regarded as particularly beautiful, as that's what this particular prefix means. Or if we see the prefix *macro-*, then we can expect something quite large. Many of these prefixes indicate a number, while others suggest a plant's size.

actino- radiating	*argo-* white
ante- before	*atro-* dark

The Enthusiast's Book of
GARDENING LATIN

bi/bis- two, twice, double	*parvi-* small
brevi- short	*pauci-* few, lacking
	poly/poli- many
calli/calo- beautiful	*post-* behind
	pre/pro- before
de- downward	*pseudo-* false
grandi- large	*quadri-* four
	quinque- five
heli- sun	
hex- six	*re-* back
hyper- above	
hypo- below	*semper -* always
	sept- seven
leuco- white	*sub-* below, somewhat, nearly
macro- large	*super-* above
magnus- large	
mille- thousand	*trans-* across
	tri- three
neo- new	
non- not	*uni-* one
octo- eight	*xero-* dry
	xylo- woody

Suffixes

Suffixes perform a similar function to prefixes, except that they come at the end of a word, rather than at the beginning. A very common suffix is -*florus* which means flowered. So for example if we see the name *jasminiflorus* we know that plant flowers like a jasmine. Sometimes a suffix will be combined with a prefix to form a complete word. An example of this is the combination of *poly-* meaning many and -*anthus* which means flower or flowered. The result is *polyanthus*, or 'many flowered'.

A lot of plants are described by what they look like or resemble, which may be other plants or entirely different objects. Therefore some common suffixes to look out for are -*aceus*, -*ineus* and -*odes*, which all mean 'resembling'.

Two other very important suffixes are -*folius* and -*phyllus*. Both these mean 'leaved', so when we see these words we know that it is the foliage of the plant that is being talked about. Remember that words may end in either -*us* or -*a*. This does not affect the meaning.

GARDENING LATIN

-aceus – resembles, like
-anthemus – flowered
-anthus – flowered
-ascens/-escens/-icens – becoming, changing to

-bundus – abundant, continually

-carpus – fruited
-cellus – diminutive, smaller

-ellus – diminutive, smaller
-ensis – place of origin
-estris – where it grows

-fer – bearing, carrying
-florus – flowered
-folius – leaved
-formis – formed, shaped

-icola – from, of, lives in
-ineus/inus – like, similar to
-iscus – diminutive, smaller

-issimus – very

-odes/-oides/-opsis/-otus – like, similar to
  -osma – fragrant, sweet-smelling
  -osus – very, large

  -phorus – carrying
  -phyllus – leaved
  - phyta – plant

  -quetrus – cornered, angled

  -rhizus – rooted

  -stemon – stamened

  -thamnus – like a shrub

Colour & Markings

To any gardener, the colour of a plant's flowers or leaves are clearly very important. This is reflected in the numerous botanical names which refer to colouring. Some of these words are easy to spot, for example *citrinus*, meaning lemon yellow, and *purpurea*, the word for purple. Some others, such as *alba*, white, and *niger*, black, have become familiar to many gardeners. Others are less obvious, and the list of colour words that follow will prove invaluable on any trip to a garden centre. The same applies to the markings on plants, which are almost as important for gardeners as the colours. An already well-known word is *variegatus* or *variegata*, meaning variegated. Other important words indicating markings include *diaphanous*, transparent, and *notatus*, spotted.

aeruginosus – rust coloured
albescens – whitish
albiflorus – has white flowers
albifrons – has white fronds
albomaculatus – has white spots
albospicus – white-spiked
albovariegatus – white variegations

albus – white
amaranticolor – amaranth coloured, purple
amethystinus – violet, amethyst
anthracinus – coal or anthracite black
aquilus – dark brown
argentatus – silvery
argenteus – silvery
atropurpureus – dark purple
atrovirens – dark green
aurantiacus – orange
aureolus – golden
aureus – golden, golden yellow
azureus – azure, sky blue

brunneus – brown

cadmicus – metallic appearance
caeruleus – blue, dark blue
caesius – lavender, bluish grey
canarius – canary yellow
carneus – flesh coloured
castus – pure, unmarked

cerasinus – cherry red
chlorus – pale or sickly green
chryseus – golden yellow
chrysophyllus – golden leaved
cinerascens – becoming ash grey
cinereus – ash grey
cinnabarinus – cinnabar red, vermilion
cinnamomeus – cinnamon brown
citrinus – lemon yellow
coccineus – scarlet
coelestis – sky blue
coerulescens – bluish
coeruleus – blue
concolor – uniformly coloured
conspersus – speckled
coracinus – raven black
corallinus – coral pink/red
croceus – saffron yellow
cupreus – copper coloured
cyaneus – Prussian blue

decolorans – discolouring, staining

deustus – scorched
diaphanus – transparent
dichromus – having two colours
dichrous – two coloured

erubescens – blushing, turning red
estriatus – without stripes
euchlorus – vibrant green

ferrugineus – rust coloured
flammeus – flaming red
flaveolus – yellowy
flavescens – pale yellow, turning yellow
flavovirens – greenish yellow
flavus – pure yellow
fucatus – painted appearance
fulginosus – sooty, dirty brown
fulvus – brownish orange, sandy coloured
fumidus – smoky grey
fuscus – brown

galbinus – yellowish, greenish yellow

glaucus – bluish-green
grammatus – raised lines
granulatus – has minute grains
griseus – grey
guttatus – spotted, speckled

helvus – light bay coloured

ianthinus/ianthus – violet
igneus – fiery red
illinitus – smudged
illustratus – painted appearance
illustris – bright
incarnatus – fleshy pink colour
iridescens – iridescent

lacteus – milk white
laetus – vivid, bright
lateritius – dark brickish red
lentiginosus – freckled
leopardinus – spotted like a leopard
lepidotus – scaly

22

The Enthusiast's Book of
GARDENING LATIN

leprosus – scaly
lilacinus – lilac coloured
lividus – lead coloured
luridus – dirty yellow
luteolus – yellowish
luteus – yellow

maculatus – spotted, blotched
margaritaceus – pearl coloured
margaritus – pearly
marginalis – with a margin, distinct edge
marmoratus – mottled
mediopictus – striped down the centre
metallicus – metallic sheen
micans – sparkling, shiny
mutabilis – changeable

niger – black
nigricans – black, blackish
niveus – snowy white
non-scriptus – unmarked
notatus – spotted, marked

occellatus – eye like
ochraceus – ochre, pale yellow
ochroleucus – pale yellow white, cream
oculatus – has eye-shaped marking
ostruthius – purplish

pallens – pale
pallidus – pale, pale green
pardinus – leopard-like spots
pavonicus/pavonius – peacock blue
pictus – painted
plumbeus – lead coloured
polystictus – many dotted
porphyreus – warm red, purple
prasinus – emerald green
punctatus – dotted
puniceus – crimson red
purpuratus/purpureus – purple

reticulatus – veined
roseus – rosy pink
rubellinus/rubellus – reddish

rubens/ruber – red
rubescens – turning red
rubicundus – rubicund, red
rufescens – almost red
rufinus – red
rufus – red, reddy brown
russatus – russet red, reddish
rutilans – red

sanguineus – blood red
scriptus – marked
sordidus – dirty
stramineus – straw coloured
subcaeruleus – a hint of blue
sulphureus – sulphur, pale yellow

variegatus – variegated
vestalis – white
vinaceus/vinosus – wine red
vinicolor – wine red
violaceus – violet
violescens – pale violet, becoming violet

virens – green
virescens – light green
viridis – green
viridissimus – very green
viridulus – greenish
virginalis/virgineus – virginal white
vitellinus – colour of egg yolk

xanthinus – yellow

Where They Grow

When we are trying to grow new plants for the first time, we need all the help we can get to ensure they are planted in the right location and in the right conditions. Sometimes, the clue to what a plant likes is in its name. For example, plants with the name *aridus*, meaning they are from very dry areas, are unlikely to thrive in boggy, shady conditions. In the same way a plant bearing the name *palustris*, meaning bog-loving, will not thank us for putting it into a rockery or in thin, dry soil. By understanding the habitat in which the plant thrives naturally, the gardener will know how to treat it in the best possible way to give it a good chance of success. In these examples, it is not so much the gardener talking to the plants – but instead the plants and their names which are talking to the gardener.

algidus – cold, mountainous
alpigenus – alpine, from high mountains
alpinus – alpine, from mountainous places
aquaticus/aquatilis – in or under water
aridus – grows in dry, arid places
arvensis – grows in cultivated land

27

calcifugus – dislikes limey areas
caliginosus – grows in misty places
campestris – grows on plains, in fields
collinus – growing on a hill
convallis – of the valley

demersus – submerged, underwater
dumetorum – of bushes, hedges
dunensis – of sand dunes

elodes – of marshes, bogs
epihydrus – grows on the water surface, floating
epigaeus/epigeios – grows in dry spots
ericetorum – of heathlands

fluitans – floating, growing on water surface
fluminensis – in running water, a river
fluvialis/fluviatilis – of the river, running water
frigidus – grows in cold regions

glacialis – from cold, glacial areas

hylaeus – of the woods
hylophilus – thrives in woodland

immersus – submerged
insularis – grows on islands
inundatus – flooded, of flooded spots

lacustris – of lakes, lagoons, ponds
latebrosus – grows in shady, dark spots
limnophilus – marsh loving
limosus – of muddy, marshy places
littoralis – of the seashore
lutarius – grows in muddy places

marinus/maritimus – of or by the sea
montanus – from mountains
muralis – growing on walls

natans – floating
nemoralis – of the woods
nivalis – growing in or near snow

oceanicus – grows near sea, ocean
orarius – grows on the shoreline
oreophilus – mountain loving
oresbius – growing on mountains

paganus – from rural, country areas
paludosus/palustris – bog or marsh loving
pastoralis – from pasture lands
peninsularis – of a peninsular
pluvialis – grows in rainy places
porophilus – grows on stony ground
potamophilus – river loving
pratensis – of meadows

riparius – grows on river banks
rivalis – of streams
rudis – of wild, uncultivated land
rupicolus – growing among rocks or cliffs
rupifragus – growing on rocks or in crevices
ruralis – of the countryside, rural areas
rusticus – from the country

sabulosus – grows in sandy places
saxatilis – grows among rocks
scopulorum – grows on rock faces
segetum – grows in cornfields
siliceus – grows on sand
silvaticus/ sylvestris – of the woods
solaris – of the sun, sunny spots
submersus – submerged

thermalis – of warm springs
trivialis – common

uliginosus – likes wet, boggy areas
urbanus – city-loving

xerophilus – of dry areas

Time & Motion

In this group of words we consider the names that tell us at what time the plants like to flower, or to open their flowers, and also in what direction the plants tend to grow. Understanding these important traits can be of enormous benefit to the gardener. Knowing whether a plant is *erectus*, upright, or *horizontalis*, horizontal, can be critical in placing it in the garden.

Meanwhile, the best-known words for flowering times are probably *annuus*, annual, and *perennis*, perennial. Some plants like to show their flowers only at night – *noctiflorus* – while others only prefer the afternoon – *pomeridianus*. Increasingly gardeners are looking for plants to brighten up the darkness of autumn and winter – in which case it is worth looking out for the words *autumnalis* and *hybernus*.

aequinoctialis – at the equinox
aestivalis – summertime
annuus – annual
ascendens – ascending
assurgens – growing upwards, ascending

biennis – biennial
brumalis – flowers in winter

cernuus – nodding, drooping
convolutus – wound or rolled together

deciduus – sheds leaves annually
declinatus – bent downwards
decumbens – lying flat but having a rising tip

epiteius – annual, yearly
erectus – upright

hesperius – evening, also Western
horizontalis – horizontal, flat on the ground
hybernalis – wintertime
hyemalis – winter

majalis – May flowering
meridianus/meridionalis – noon, midday

noctiflorus – flowers at night
nudiflorus – flowers before leaves show
nutans – swaying

oporinus – late summer, autumn

patens – spreading
pendulus – hanging down, drooping
pensilis – hanging, overhanging
perennis – perennial
pomeridianus – afternoon
praecox – very early flowering, premature
prenans – drooping

radians – radiating outwards
radiatus – spreading rays, radiating
reclinatus – reclined, leaning
rectus – straight, upright
recurvus – bent or curved backwards
reflexus – bent back
revolutus – rolled backwards

scandens – growing upwards, climbing
seclusus – hidden, secluded
sempervirens – evergreen
serotinus – late, late season
solstitialis – midsummer, summer solstice
supinus – supine, flat
suspensus/suspendus – hanging

tardus – late
tortilis – twisted
tortuosus – twisted
trimestris – matures in three months

velox – fast growing
veris – spring
vernalis/vernus – spring
vespertinus – flowers in the evening

Where in the World

In the same way that we can learn from a plant's natural habitat, gardeners can also benefit from knowing from which country or place a plant comes. We can guess that a plant called *africanus* – from Africa – may not appreciate some of the cooler parts of the British Isles in winter. On the other hand any plant named *japonicus* or *japonica* is probably well-used to the changing seasons that its native land provides, while a plant called *fennicus* – from Finland – may relish even colder conditions. Common words in this category include *orientalis*, meaning from the East or oriental, and *australiensis*, telling us the plant comes from Australia. A very popular plant in recent years has been *Verbena bonariensis*, its name informing us that this striking perennial originates in Buenos Aires, in Argentina. Many plants also bear the name *chinensis*, *sinensis* or *sinicus*, all of them indicating it comes from that great home of wonderful flora, China.

aethiopicus – African, Ethiopian
afer – North African
afghanica – Afghan
africanus – African

aleppicus – from Aleppo, Syria
alexandrinus – from Alexandria, Egypt
alienus – foreign
amazonicus – from the Amazon
americanus – American
anglicus – English
antipodus – Antipodean
arabicus – Arabian
australiensis – Australian
australis – southern, of the Southern Hemisphere
austriacus – Austrian

bonariensis – from Buenos Aires, Argentina
bononiensis – from Bologna, Italy
borealis – northern
britannicus – from Britain

californicus – Californian
cashmerianus – Kashmiri
centralis – central
chinensis – Chinese
cornubiensis – Cornish

dalmaticus – Dalmatian
damascenus – from Damascus
delphicus – from Delphi, Greece
dumnoniensis – Devonian

europeus/europaeus – European
exoniensis – from Exeter

fennicus – Finnish

gallicus – French
garganicus – from Gargano, Italy
germanicus – German
graecus – Greek

hellenicus – Greek
helveticus – Swiss
himalayense – Himalayan
hispanicus – Spanish
hollandicus – Dutch
hyperboreus – from the far north

ibiricus – from the Iberian peninsula
indicus – Indian
islandicus – Icelandic
italicus – Italian

japonicus – Japanese

kewensis – from Kew Gardens
koreanus – Korean

limensis – from Lima, Peru
lusitanicus – Portuguese

moldavicus – Moldavian

neapolitanus – from Naples
niliacus/niloticus – from the Nile Valley
novae-zelandiae – New Zealand

occidentalis – western
orientalis – eastern

persicus – Persian
polaris – from the North Pole
punica – from Carthage
pyrenaeus/pyrenaicus – Pyrenees

scoticus – Scottish
sinensis/sinicus – Chinese
syriacus – Syrian

tauricus – from the Crimea
thibeticus – Tibetan

virginianus – from Virginia

Shape & Size

Will the plant grow tall or stay small? Will it have rounded leaves or sharp, pointed foliage? Many of the specific names of plants give clues to their shapes and size. Some words are more obvious than others. The name *giganteus*, for example, meaning gigantic, gives a clear idea of how big a species might become. Meanwhile the name *minimus* equally clearly tells us the plant may be on the small side. A frequently-used word meaning dwarf is *nanus*, another is *parvus* meaning small, while *magnus* indicates a large size. A plant with rounded leaves may be called *rotundifolius*, while one with twisted stems or leaves may bear the name *contortus*. For many the word *grandiflorus* will be a welcome sign – it means the plant has large flowers or is free-flowering.

acaulis – without a stem
aculeatus – prickly
acutus – sharp pointed
aduncus – hooked
aggregatus – clustered flowers
alatus – winged
alternans/alternatus – alternate leaves

angularis – angled, angular
angustus – narrow
annularis – ring shaped
aphyllus – leafless

bifidus – forked or cleft leaves
biflorus – two flowers
bifoliatus/bifolius – two leaves
bisectus – cut in two sections
blepharophyllus – fringed leaves
brachyanthus – short-flowered
brachypetalus – short-petalled
brachypodus – short-stalked
brevis – short
bulbosus – bulbous

caespitosus – tufted
calcaratus – spurred, horned
calceolatus – shoe shaped
campanulatus – bell-shaped flowers
capillipes – slender stalk
capitellatus – with small heads

capreolatus – with tendrils, twining
caudatus – tailed, with a tail-like part
chirophyllus – hand shaped leaves
ciliaris/ciliatus – fringed
cocciferus – with berries
cochlearis – spoon-shaped
comosus – hairy, tufted
conjunctus/conjugatus – joined together, connected
constrictus – erect, dense
contortus – twisted
cordatus – heart shaped
cordifolius – heart shaped leaves
cornutus – horned
coronatus – crowned
crassus – thick
crispatus/crispus – curled

deflexus – bent sharply downwards
dentatus – toothed
difformis – of unusual shape, misshapen
diffusus – spreading loosely
digitatus/digitalis – fingered

diphyllus – two leaved

elatus – tall
elongatus – lengthened, elongated
ellipticus – elliptical, elliptically shaped
emarginatus – leaves which are notched at top
or apex
ensatus – sword-like
erectus – upright
erinaceus – prickly
exaltatus/exaltus – very tall
excelsior – very tall

fastigiatus – erect, upright branches
fissifolius – split leaves
flabellatus – fan shaped
flagellum – whip or tail shaped
flexuosus – winding, wavy
flore-pleno – double flowered
frutescens – like a shrub
furcans/furcatus – forked

giganteus – very big, gigantic
gigas – giant
globosus – round, globular
globularis – ball shaped, small spheres
gracilis – slender, graceful
grandiflorus – large flowered
grandifolius – large leaves
grandis – big, showy

hastatus – arrow or spear shaped
hastilis – spear-like
humilis – low growing, dwarf

imbricatus – overlapping
incisus – deeply cut
inconspicuus – small
intactus – unopened

jubatus – crested

labiatus – with a developed lip, lip shaped
linearifolius – linear leaves

GARDENING LATIN

linearis – narrow, linear
lobatus – with lobes
lobularis – with lobes
locustus – thorny
longus – long
lophanthus – crested flower

macellus – lean, meagre
magnificus – magnificent
magnus – large
major/majus – larger, greater
maximus – largest
medius – medium sized
megarrhizus – has large roots
minimus – smallest
minor/minus – small
minutus – very small
mucronatus – sharp edged or tipped
multiceps – many headed

nanus – dwarf
nanellus – very dwarf

---

nervosus – veined, sinewy
numismatus – coin shaped
nummularis/nummularius – coin shaped, round

obesus – fat
oblatus – oval shaped
obtusatus – blunt

palmatus – palm shaped
parvulus – very small, dwarf
parvus – small
pauciflorus – few flowers
pelviformis – basin shaped
pennatus – feathered
petiolatis – has a leaf stalk
pinnatus – like a feather in form
platypus – has a broad stalk, foot
pleniflorus – multi-flowered, double flowers
plumosus – feathery
polygyrus – twining
ponderosus – large, heavy
praealtus – very tall

47

procerus – tall
prodigiosus – enormous, wonderful, prodigious
profusus – profuse, abundant in flower or fruit
prolificus – abundant in flower or fruit
prostratus – low lying, prostrate
pumilus – dwarf
pusillus – very small, insignificant
pungens – sharp pointed
pygmaeus – pygmy
pyriformis – pear shaped

racemosus – flowers forming in racemes, clusters
radiosus – having many rays
repens – creeping
reptans – creeping
ringens – open-mouthed
rosularis – has rosettes
rotatus – wheel shaped
rotundatus – rounded
rotundifolius – rounded leaves

scutellatus – dish shaped

sessiflorus – stalkless flowers
sessilis – stalkless
sphaericus – spherical
sphaerocephalus – round headed
stamineus – prominent stamens
stellaris/stellatus – star shaped

tenuiflorus – slender flowers
tenuifolius – slender leaves
tenuis – slender
tubaeformis – trumpet shaped
tubiflorus – trumpet shaped flowers
tumidus – swollen

umbellatus – umbrella-shaped flowers, umbels

vescus – thin, weak

Smell, Touch & Taste

Though our eyes are important in judging a plant's value, we sometimes need to use other senses as well. The names of plants can tell us whether they are sweet-smelling – as well as the opposite – whether they are smooth, hairy or thorny, or even whether they have a bitter taste. Two important names in this group here are the self-explanatory *fragrans*, and the less pleasant *foetidus* – which tells us the plant stinks. Another common word in this context is *odoratus*, which perhaps contrary to expectations indicates the plant is sweet-smelling. But we may want to steer clear of anything called *hircinus* ... it means it smells like a goat. We should also be cautious with anything described as *ferox* or *armatus* – they indicate it is prickly. There is better news for a plant which has the word *cibarius* in its name, as this suggests it is edible.

acris – acrid
adenophyllus – has leaves with sticky glands, hairs
adpressus – lying flat, as in hairs on a stem
altilis – fat, nutritious
amarus – bitter
anacanthus – without thorns

anisatum – anise scented
armatus – thorny
aromaticus – fragrant
asper – rough
asperifolius – rough-leaved

barbatus – bearded
barbellata – has small barbs
bombyciferum /bombycinus – silky
brevisetus – short bristled

calvus – bald, hairless
causticus – caustic
ceraceus – waxy
cerefolius – waxy leaved
cibarius – edible
ciliaris – fringed with soft hairs
citrodorus – lemon-scented
coriaceus – leathery
corrugatus – wrinkled, furrowed

dealbatus – covered with white powder

---

detonsus – clipped, bald
dulcis – sweet, mild

edulis – edible
emeticus – emetic, causing vomiting
eriacanthus – woolly-spined
erianthus – woolly flowers
eriophorus – woolly
esculentus – tasty, edible

farinosus – powdery like sprinkled flour
felosmus – foul-smelling
ferox – prickly, thorny
fimbriatus – fringed
foetidus – stinking
fragrans – fragrant
fragrantissimus – very sweet-smelling
fulgens – shiny, glistening

glaber – smooth
glaberrimus – very smooth

glaucus – covered in a bloom
graveolens – heavily scented

hedys – sweet aroma or taste
hircinus – smells like a goat
hirsutus – hairy
hirtus – hairy
hispidus – with bristles

imberbis – without hairs or spines
inebrians – intoxicating
inodorus – without scent
irritans – irritating, causes a rash

laciniatus – torn, jagged
laevigatus – smooth
lanatus – woolly
lanosus – woolly
lanuginosus – downy
lucidus – shiny

mollis – soft
moschatus – musky scent
mucosus – slimy

nauseosus – nauseating
nitens – shining
nitidus – shiny

odoratus/odorus – fragrant
olidus – smelly
oxyacanthus – with very sharp thorns

papyraceus – papery texture
phu – bad-smelling
pilosus – with soft long hairs
plumosus – feathery
ptarmicus – causes sneezing
pubens/pubescens – downy
pungens – pungent
purgans – purgative

rugosus – wrinkled

saccharinus – sweet
scaber – rough
scaberrimus – very rough
spicatus – with spikes
striatus – striped
suaveolens – sweet-smelling
suavis – sweet
succulentus – juicy, fleshy

tormentosus – very hairy, very woolly
tragophyllus – leaves with a goat-like smell

viscidus – sticky
viscosus – sticky

In memoriam

As in other branches of science, botanists and horticulturalists sometimes just can't resist naming newly identified species after people, either real or imaginary. Some plants take their names from great botanists or plant collectors of the past. The word *banksii* is employed for plants named after Sir Joseph Banks (1743–1820), a naturalist who sailed with Captain Cook, while *forrestii* signifies the plant is name after the Scottish-born plant collector George Forrest (1873–1932). Other names have a more classical theme, such as the genus *Achillea*, named after the Greek hero of the Trojan wars, Achilles. Others still are named after royalty, ancient gods, the wives of botanists – and of course other botanists and gardeners as well. For example, botanist Julia Mlokosewitsch gave her name to the lovely yellow peony she discovered *Paeonia mlokosewitschii*.

> *Achillea* – Achilles
> *ajacis* – Ajax
> *Andromeda* – Andromeda, princess rescued by Perseus
> *armandii* – l'Abbé Armand David, French botanist
> *Artemisia* – Artemisia, Queen of Caria, also Artemis the
> Greek goddess

banksianus – Joseph Banks, British botanist and explorer
banksii – Joseph Banks
Barbarae – Saint Barbara

danfordiae – Mrs CG Danford
davidii – l'Abbé Armand David
Dianthus – the flower of the Greek god Zeus
douglasii – David Douglas, British plant collector

ecae – Mrs EC Aitchison

falconeri – Hugh Falconer
fargesii – Paul Guillaume Farges
farrerae – Mrs Farrer
farreri – Reginald Farrer
flora – Flora, Roman goddess of flowering plants
florindae – Florinda N Thompson
forrestii – George Forrest, British plant collector

georgii – George Forrest

halleri – Hans Hallier

Helenium – Helen of Troy
hilairei – Saint Hilaire
hodgsonii – BH Hodgson
hookerae – Lady Hooker
Humea – Lady Amelia Hume
hugonis – Father Hugo Scallon

imperatricis – Empress Josephine

jackmanii – George Jackman
jonesii – Jones
juliae – Julia Mlokosewitsch, botanist
julianae – Juliana Schneider

kelloggii – Albert Kellogg, American
botanist

luciliae – Lucile Boissier, wife of Swiss
botanist Edmond Boissier

menziesii – Archibald Menzies
mlokosewitschii – Julia Mlokosewitsch

narcissus – Narcissus, beautiful Greek youth
punished by the gods

Paeonia – Paeon, Greek healer whom Zeus rescued
by turning into a flower
Pandorea – Pandora
Protea – Proteus, the sea god

reginae-olga – Queen Olga
robbiae – Mrs Robb
robertianus – Robert

smithii – Smith

victoria – Queen Victoria

wardii – Frank Kingdom-Ward, British botanist
williamsii – Williams
willmottianus – Ellen Willmott, gardener
Wisteria – Caspar Wistar, American doctor
wrightii – Robert Wright

The Good, the Bad and the Ugly

As well giving botanical descriptions of a plant's colour, shape or size, some species' names offer more of a personal opinion about the plant in question. Words such as charming, bland, wonderful and so on may not be very scientific, but they do give us an idea of what to expect. We would naturally be drawn to plants which are elegant, *elegans*, graceful, *gracilis*, or simply wonderful, *mirabilis*. We may be more wary, on the other hand, of plants which sound weak, *debilis*, insignificant, *pusillus*, or just plain dull, *tristis*. A frequently used word for plants is *vulgaris*, which however does not mean 'vulgar' in the usual sense, but common or usual. A similar word is *communis*, which also means ordinary. In contrast, a name with the word *singularis* tells you it is a one-off.

> *adulterinus* – not pure, not genuine
> *amabilis* – beautiful, lovely
> *ambiguous* – ambiguous, of doubtful classification
> *amoenus* – attractive, charming
> *anomalus* – anomalous, unusual
>
> *bellidifolius* – has beautiful leaves

bellus – handsome, beautiful
benedictus – blessed
blandus – charming, mild
bonus – good

callianthus – has beautiful flowers
callicarpus – has beautiful fruit
callistemon – beautiful stamens in flower
callistus – beautiful
calophyllus – has beautiful leaves
communis – grows in a group
concinnus – neat, attractive

debilis – weak, feeble
decoratus – decorative
decorus – elegant
delectus – chosen, choice
delicatus – delicate, tender
dubius – uncertain, dubious
durabilis – durable, lasting

elegans – elegant

elegantissumus – most elegant
excelsior – noble, taller

fallax – deceptive, false
fecundus – fertile, fruitful
feris – wild
flaccidus – limp, feeble
floribundus – free-flowering
floridus – free-flowering
formosus – handsome, beautiful

generalis – normal, as expected
gracilis – graceful, slender

hypochondriacus – melancholy

illustris – bright, brilliant
imperialis – showy
impudicus – impudent, shameful
infestus – may infest, be invasive
inodorus – scentless
insanus – insane

insignis – remarkable, distinguished

magnificus – magnificent
mirabilis – marvellous, wonderful
mirandus – remarkable
mixtus – mixed
modestus – modest
monstrosus – abnormal size or shape
mutabilis – variable, fickle

nudus – naked, bare

obscurus – obscure, gloomy
occultus – hidden
ornans – showy, splendid

paradoxus – strange
peregrinus – exotic
perfectus – complete
permixtus – confusing, mixed up
plenus – double, full
prodigiosus – marvellous, prodigious

profusus – profuse in flowering
prolificus – prolific, in fruit or flowers
pulchellus – pretty
pulcher – beautiful
pusillus – insignificant

regalis – royal, regal
regius – kingly
robustus – robust

sacrorum – sacred
sanctus – holy
simplex – simple
singularis – distinct, singular, one-off
solidus – dense
sparsus – few
speciosus – showy
spectabilis – spectacular, showy
spectandrus – showy
sphacelatus – withered, appears dead
spurious – false
sterilis – sterile, barren

The Enthusiast's Book of
GARDENING LATIN

superbus – superb, proud

tristis – sad, bitter, dull
triumphans – triumphant
trivialis – common, ordinary

urens – stinging

venenatus – poisonous
venustus – charming
verus – true, standard
vulgaris – common

Looks Like

A large number of plants or parts of plants are described by what they resemble. This may be other plants, fruit, vegetables, mammals or even reptiles. For example, a plant called *buxifolius* will have leaves like those of the box plant and something named *camelliiflorus* will have flowers like those of a camellia. More exotically, a name featuring *leopardinius* will indicate that the plant is leopard-spotted and *hystrix* tells us that it is prickly like a porcupine. Quite a common word is *dens-canis* which means that the plant — or part of it — resembles a dog's tooth. Rather more unusual is the description *ornithorhynchus* — which means the plant is shaped like a bird's beak.

If we consider the colour of a plant, the word *leonis* indicates it is coloured like a lion. On the same theme, the word *tigrinus* tells us that part of the plant or its flower has stripes like a tiger's, while the description *cochleatus* means it is twisted rather like the spiral on the shell of a snail. Perhaps one of the most evocative is *superciliaris* which suggests the plant is shaped like an eyebrow. Meanwhile, one of the oddest of all is the word *saurocephalus*, which means the plant has a head like a lizard. Plant names really do tell some strange stories.

adonidifolius – leaves like *Adonis*, fennel-like
aesculifelius – almond-like
althaeoides – like hollyhock
amaranthoides – resembling *Amaranth*
arborescens – becoming tree-like
arboreus – tree-like
arundinaceus – like a reed or cane
azaleoides – like an *Azalea*

bellidifolius – daisy-like leaves
betulinus – birch-like
botryoides – like a bunch of grapes
bucephalus – ox-headed
buxifolius – leaves like box, *Buxus*

camelliiflorus – flowers like the *Camellia*
citratus – citrus-like
citriodorus – lemon-scented
cochleatus – twisted like a snail's shell
colombinus – dove-like, flowers shaped like doves
conoideus – cone-like
corneus – horn-like

cupressinus – like cypress
cypreus – like copper

daucoides – like the carrot, *Daucus*
delphinifolius – leaves like the *Delphinium*
dens-canis – shaped like a dog-tooth
dryophyllus – oak-like leaves

elephantum – of elephants, huge
equinus – of horses
ericoides – heath-like

fagifolius – leaves like the beech
ferulaceus – leaves like fennel
filicinus – fern-like
fragarioides – like the strawberry plant

genistifolius – leaves like broom, *Genista*
gorgoneus – snake-haired
gramineus – like grass

hederaceus – like ivy

hederifolius – ivy-shaped leaves
helianthoides – resembling sunflowers
hepatica – resembling shape or colour of liver
hypnoides – like moss
hystrix – like a porcupine

iodes – like violet, *Viola*
iridiflorus – has flowers like an *Iris*

jasmineus – like jasmine
jonquilla – leaves like rushes
junceus – like a rush
juniperifolius – has leaves like juniper

lagenarius – bottle-shaped
laurinus – like laurel
lavandulaceus – like lavender
leonis – coloured like a lion
leonurus – like a lion's tail
leopardinus – leopard-spotted
liliiflorus – flowers like lilies

lotoides – like a lotus

meloformis – melon-shaped
meniscifolius – crescent-shaped leaves
morifolius – leaves like a mulberry
myuros – with a mouse tail

nepetoides – like catnip
nidus – nest-like

oleoides – like the olive, *Olea*
orchideus/orchioides – resembling orchids
ornithocephalus – like a bird's head
ornithopodus – shaped like a bird's foot
ornithorhynchus – like a bird's beak
ostreatus – as if it were covered in oyster shells

palliatus – like a hooded cloak
papillionaceus – like a butterfly
pedatus – shaped like a foot
petaloideus – like a petal

pineus – pine-like
piperita – like peppermint
placentiformis – shaped like a cake
pomaceus – resembling an apple
populifolius – leaves like the poplar
porcinus – relating to pigs
primuloides – like a primrose
proboscideus – like a long snout or nose
psycodes – resembling butterflies
pyriformis – shaped like a pear

quercifolius – leaves like an oak

ranunculoides – resembling the buttercup
reniformis – shaped like a kidney

sagittalis – arrow-like
salicinus – willow-like
sambucifolius – leaves like the elder
sarcodes – like flesh
saurocephalus – head like a lizard
scorpioides – like a scorpion

scutum – like a small shield
setaceus – bristle-like
similis – like, similar to
simulans – similar to
strobilaceus – like a cone
superciliaris – shaped like an eyebrow

tabulaeformis – like a table
taurinus – bull-like
tigrinus – striped like a tiger

urticoides – like a nettle

vermiculatus – worm-like

Common Plants

In this section we look at the common names for some of the most popular plants in Britain, and give them their full botanical names. The names of some different varieties of these well-known plants are also given, as well as the origin and meaning of the names where appropriate. Where a plant's genus name is repeated, it has been shortened to a capital letter followed by a full stop. For example when writing about the genus *Viola*, this can be shortened simply to *V.*

African blue lily This charming plant is also well known by its botanical name, *Agapanthus*. As its popular name suggests, *Agapanthus* comes from Africa but more and more cultivated varieties are being adapted to the colder climate of Britain. These include the cultivars *A.* 'Dorothy Palmer' and *A.* 'Alice Gloucester'.

Apple The trees which bear this fruit all belong to the genus called *Malus*. Species of *Malus* have been cultivated for centuries for their fruit, though some members of the genus are grown mainly for their superb flowers. These include *M. floribunda* and the stunning *M.* 'Lemoinei'.

Bamboo Bamboos are a familiar sight in many British gardens. They are part of the group of plants called Bambusoideae, a sub-family of the grass family Gramineae. There are a number of different genera of bamboo, including *Bambusa*, *Chusquea* and *Phyllostachys*. Familiar species include *Chusquea culeou* and *Phyllostachys flexuosa* (Zigzag bamboo).

Bay tree The bay tree or sweet bay is known scientifically as *Laurus nobilis*, which means well known or outstanding. It is part of the small genus *Laurus*, which contains just two species.

Beech This very common British tree is of the genus *Fagus*. The botanical name for the Common beech is *F. sylvatica*. The full name for the stunning Copper beech is *F. sylvatica f. purpurea* (the f. shows that this is simply a different *form* of the common beech with coppery leaves, not a different species).

Birch The birch, which remains a favourite tree in Britain, is the common name for the genus *Betula*. The elegant silver birch is known as *B. pendula*, the name referring to the drooping shoots of the tree rather than its silvery colour.

Blackthorn This beautiful but prickly tree, which is also called sloe, is part of the genus *Prunus* and is known as *Prunus spinosa*. The name means it is 'full of spines'. The group *Prunus* includes the wonderfully-flowered cherry trees.

Bluebell This is the well-known name for a small group of plants called *Hyacinthoides*, the name meaning they resemble *Hyacinthus*. The English bluebell's botanical name is *Hyacinthoides non-scriptus* (meaning unmarked) while the name of the slightly paler and more vigorous Spanish bluebell is *Hyacinthoides hispanica*.

Box This practical group of plants, which are often used for hedges and topiary, are known botanically as *Buxus*. The Common box is called *B. sempervirens*, meaning evergreen, as indeed all *Buxus* species are. Another popular species is the small-leaved box, *B. microphylla*.

Broom The name commonly used for the genus of shrubs and trees *Genista*. A well-known species is *G. aetnensis*, known as Mount Etna broom. Confusingly, broom is also the name for shrubs of the popular genus *Cytisus*. *C. scoparius* is Common broom, and there are a number of cultivars such as *C.* 'Windlesham Ruby'.

Buttercup The familiar buttercup or crowfoot is part of the genus *Ranunculus*. Though the creeping buttercup *R. repens* can be a problem for lawns, a number of buttercups are cultivated for their brilliant flowers. One cultivar, with pure white flowers, is *R. aconitifolius* 'Flore Pleno'.

Butterfly bush This butterfly-attracting shrub is called *Buddleja davidii* in honour of a French botanist Armand David, and is part of the genus *Buddleja*. An attractive cultivar is *B. davidii* 'Black Knight'. Most plants in this genus attract butterflies though some, such as *B. asiatica*, flower in late winter when no butterflies are to be seen. When not used scientifically buddleja is sometimes spelt with an 'i' rather than a 'j'.

Carnation The carnation has been cultivated since at least Roman times. Its species name is *Dianthus caryophyllus* but there are many cultivars. These include *D.* 'Bookham Fancy' and *D.* 'Clara'.

Cherry trees The stunning flowering cherry trees are part of the large genus *Prunus*. The Japanese in particular have admired their delightful blossom for at least 5,000 years. The species name for the wild cherry is *P. avium* which means 'of the birds' – many birds are very fond of the flower buds. A popular cultivar is *P. avium* 'Plena'.

Christmas rose The Christmas rose is known botanically as *Helleborus niger*, and as its common name suggests this plant flowers in the winter. It is thought the Romans may have introduced it to Britain. Another species *H. orientalis* is often referred to as the Lenten rose.

Chrysanthemum One of the most popular plants around the world, and sometimes referred to just as 'mum', the name *Chrysanthemum* is also the name of the genus. The very popular cultivated varieties were briefly re-named under the genus *Dendranthema* some years ago but this name change was largely ignored by gardeners – and now they have been restored once again as *Chrysanthemum*. The name means literally 'gold flowered' though they now come in many different colours, as well as different shapes and sizes.

Clematis A common name for the genus *Clematis* is Old man's beard, though most gardeners now usually use the name clematis. This genus is divided into three distinct groups based on when they flower, their habits and pruning requirements.

Clover The botanical name for clover is *Trifolium*, a large genus of more than 230 species – the name means three-leaved. An attractive variety is *T. repens* 'Purpurascens', with the name 'repens' indicating its creeping qualities.

Columbine This familiar cottage garden plant rejoices in the botanical name *Aquilegia*. The species *A. vulgaris* (meaning common) which is sometimes known as Granny's bonnet, is a native of Britain. An attractive alternative is a closely related genus *Semiaquilegia*, of which *S. ecalcarata* is a popular example.

Coneflower The name coneflower is applied to not just one but two different groups of plants – the genus *Echinacea*, and also the genus *Rudbeckia*. Both are closely related members of the daisy family, Compositae. The most popular species of *Echinacea* is probably *E. purpurea*, which as its name suggests is purple, and which has cultivars such as *E. purpurea* 'Robert Bloom'. The best-known species of *Rudbeckia* is perhaps *R. fulgida* (meaning shining) which is also known as Black-eyed Susan.

Cowslip This well-known plant's botanical name is *Primula veris*, making it part of the genus *Primula*. Though familiar as a wild plant, it is often grown in gardens for early spring colour. 'Veris' means Spring.

Cranesbill This old name is for the well-known genus *Geranium*. There are around 300 species of Geranium in the world, and many cultivated varieties – probably because they are both attractive and relatively easy to grow. Typical examples include *G. clarkei* 'Kashmir Purple' and *G. sylvaticum* 'Mayflower'. The genus *Geranium* is closely related to the more frost-sensitive genus *Pelargonium*, whose plants are – confusingly – sometimes known commonly as geraniums.

Daffodil The popular name for the genus of flowers known as *Narcissus*. Daffodils come in a wide variety of shapes and sizes, so much so that the genus is divided into twelve different divisions, depending on their flower shape. Division one, for example, is called the Trumpet division and the flowers have a trumpet which is as long or longer than the petals. By no means all are the familiar yellow. Some species, for example *N. cantabricus*, whose name indicates it is from the Cantabrian Mountains of Spain, can be a delicate milky white colour.

Dahlia The dahlia originates from Central America and is now one of the most cultivated plants in the world. There are around 28 species of Dahlia, but the vast array of cultivars come mostly from just two, *D. coccinea* and *D. pinnata*. They are formed into ten different groups, based on the shape of their flowers; Single, Anemone, Collerette, Water-lily, Decorative, Ball, Pompon, Cactus, Semi-cactus and Miscellaneous.

Daisy The daisy frequently found on our lawns is *Bellis perennis*, a species which itself has led to cultivars such as *B. perennis* 'Pomponette'. There are also other plants popularly called daisies, such as the Shasta daisy. This comes from a different genus and thus has a different name, *Leucanthemum* x *superbum*.

Delphinium This is also the botanical name for this group of plants, the genus *Delphinium*. There are many popular cultivars of this genus, most of them from the species *Delphinium elatum*, for example *D.* 'Blue Nile' and *D.* 'Gillian Dallas'.

Dogwood The shrubs and trees known as dogwood belong to the group *Cornus*. An increasingly popular species is *C. florida*, which has a number of cultivars including *C. florida* 'Apple Blossom'.

Elder These shrubs and trees are known scientifically as *Sambucus*. The Common elder is *S. nigra*, while *S. nigra* 'Aurea' is known as the Golden elder. A new and stunning elder is *S. nigra* 'Black Lace'.

Ferns There are many different genera of fern, from *Athyrium* and *Dryopteris* to *Osmunda* and *Woodsia*. The popular Lady fern's botanical name is *Athyrium filix-femina* while the elegant Hart's tongue fern is *Asplenium scolopendrium*. Tree ferns are becoming increasingly common in British gardens and conservatories – the species *Dicksonia Antarctica* and *Cyathea australis* being among the most popular.

Forget-me-not These charming plants are from the genus *Myosotis*. The species most used for cultivation is *M. sylvatica*. Another species *M. scorpioides*, the Water forget-me-not, can be used as a marginal water plant for ponds or boggy areas.

Foxglove Still common in the wild, this increasingly popular garden plant is from the genus *Digitalis*. The Common foxglove is *D. purpurea*, reflecting the plant's usual purple colour, though there are now white and orange forms. The plant grown to extract the powerful heart stimulant digitalis, which is present in most species, is *D. lanata*.

Fuchsia This very popular genus of plants is named in honour of a sixteenth-century German botanist called Leonhard Fuchs (1501–1566). The genus *Fuchsia* was in fact first identified by a French botanist Father Charles Plumier on a Caribbean island at the end of the seventeenth century. He named the plant after the botanist Fuchs whose work he admired. The German, of course, had never seen the plant.

Gentian These beautifully flowered plants are from the substantial genus *Gentiana*, which contains more than 350 species. Many of these are alpine species and are prized for their lovely blue flowers. A favourite one is *G. sino-ornata*, its name indicating both that it is an attractive plant and from China.

Geranium See Cranesbill

Gladioli This ever-popular plant is often referred to commonly as 'gladioli'. But in fact these plants are from the genus *Gladiolus*. The plural form 'gladioli' has somehow become the name that most people use. Technically one should not refer to 'a gladioli' but rather 'a gladiolus'. The genus is divided into two groups, Grandiflorus and Primulinus, the former having much longer flower heads.

Grass Grasses belong to the family Gramineae in which there are many different genera, including *Briza*, *Deschampsia*, *Festuca*, *Spartina* and *Stipa*. Two popular ornamental grasses include *Festuca glauca* and *Miscanthus sacchariflorus*. There are a number of different species of grass which have been cultivated for use in garden lawns and for sports grounds. These include perennial ryegrass, *Lolium perenne*, varieties of red fescue, *festuca rubra*, and smooth-stalked meadow grass, *Poa pratensis*.

Hart's tongue fern See Ferns

Hazel These trees and shrubs belong to the genus *Corylus*. An interesting variety is *C. avellana* 'Contorta', the well-named corkscrew hazel.

Hawthorn The hawthorn, also called may, belongs to the large genus *Crataegus* which contains around 170 species. The common hawthorn is C. *monogyna*, while an attractive pink-flowered variety is *C. laevigata* 'Paul's Scarlet'.

Honeysuckle The genus name for the honeysuckle is *Lonicera*. Many species are of course prized for their scent, especially, as its name suggests, *L. fragrantissima*. There are now more than a hundred cultivated varieties of honeysuckle; another favourite is *L. periclymenum* 'Graham Thomas'.

Holly The holly tree is part of a genus known as *Ilex*. The common holly shrub or tree is *I. aquifolium*, meaning it has pointed leaves. Though we associate the name holly with an evergreen plant, some species of *Ilex* are deciduous, such as *I. verticillata*, whose common name is Winterberry.

Hollyhock An ever-present plant in the cottage garden, the hollyhock's scientific name is *Alcea*. The common hollyhock A. *rosea* is widely cultivated, and in fact does not occur naturally in the wild. An unusual dark-flowered variety is *A. rosea* 'Nigra'. The genus *Alcea* is closely related to the genus *Althaea*, and in fact *Alcea rosea* is sometimes called *Althaea rosea*. The species *Althaea offic-inalis* is known as the marsh mallow.

Iceland poppy See Poppy

Iris Gardeners already use the botanical name for the genus *Iris*. Irises are divided into different botanical groups, the most popular of them including the bearded irises. These are so called because of the dense hairs or 'beard' on the flower petals. There are many cultivated varieties of bearded irises – many coming from the species *I. pallida*.

Ivy The genus name for the evergreen ivy is *Hedera*. The Common English ivy is *H. helix* which has a number of cultivars including *H. helix* 'Manda's Crested' and *H. helix* 'Atropurpurea', whose leaves turn deep purple in winter.

Japonica The scientific name for Japonica or flowering quince is *Chaenomeles*, a small genus with only a few species. One species is called *C. japonica*, but the best-known and most often cultivated japonica is actually *C. speciosa* – which in fact comes from China.

Jasmine These shrubs and climbers make up the genus *Jasminum*. Common jasmine is *J. officinale*. The striking yellow jasmine is called *J. humile*, while the Royal jasmine is well named as *J. grandiflorum* – meaning free flowering.

Kingcup The Kingcup, sometimes also called the marsh marigold, is known botanically as *Caltha palustris*, the second name indicating it likes boggy areas. An attractive variety is called *C. palustris* 'Flore Plena'.

Lavender The botanical name for this fragrant plant is *Lavandula*. The common name French lavender refers to the species *L. dentata*, as well as *L. stoechas*. This latter one is also often called Spanish lavender.

Leylandii This has become the widely-used name for the famously – or some would say infamously – fast-growing conifer tree, the Leyland cypress. The correct species name is x *Cupressocyparis leylandii*. The 'x' coming before the two names indicates it is a hybrid between two different genera, the Monterey cypress *Cupressus macrocarpa* and the Alaska Cedar *Chamaecyparis nootkatensis* . There are a number of varieties, including x *C. leylandii* 'Harlequin' and x *C. leylandii* 'Castlewellan'.

Lilac These beautiful and often fragrant shrubs and trees are from the genus *Syringa*. Many of the varieties come from the common lilac, *S. vulgaris*, which has been cultivated since the sixteenth century. They include *S.* 'Mme Antoine Buchner' and *S.* 'Blue Hyacinth'.

Lily The lily is the common name for the genus of plants *Lilium*. It is also the name sometimes used generally for the family of plants called Liliaceae – of which *Lilium* is just one member. So for example the genus of flowers called *Convallaria* – also part of the same Liliaceae family – are known popularly as Lily-of-the-valley.

Love-in-a-mist These charming annuals are from the genus *Nigella*. The botanical name for love-in-a-mist is *N. damascena*, its name telling us its origins are from around Damascus in Syria. Beautiful cultivated varieties of this include *N. damascena* 'Persian Jewels'. A slightly different but related and very striking plant is *N. papillosa*, whose flowers are purple.

Lupin The common name is similar to the genus name, *Lupinus*. Although best-known as herbaceous perennials or annuals, some species are shrubs, including the Tree lupin *L. arboreus*.

Maple Maple trees are increasingly well-known by their botanical name *Acer*. The word comes the Latin for 'sharp' as acers were apparently good for making spears. The sycamore, *Acer pseudoplatanus*, is part of the same genus, its name meaning 'false plane'. The species *A. palmatum* is the Japanese maple, and there are many beautiful varieties, including *A. palmatum* 'Bloodgood'.

Marigold The name marigold can be a little confusing for gardeners. In Europe the name refers to the genus *Calendula*, with *C. officinalis*, the common or pot marigold, the best known. In America and other parts of the world, however, marigold refers to a different genus – *Tagetes*. French marigolds (*T. patula*) and African marigolds (*T. erecta*) are popular bedding plants. Plants were named marigold after Mary's Gold, in honour of the Virgin Mary. For marsh marigold see Kingcup.

Michaelmas daisy These long-flowering garden favourites belong to the genus *Aster*. The name Michaelmas daisy usually refers to a small number of *Aster* species, especially *A. novae-angliae* and *A. novi-belgii* and their cultivars. Popular varieties include *A. novae-angliae* 'Harrington's Pink' and *A. novi-belgii* 'Jenny'. Michaelmas Day is on 29 September, and the common name refers to the plant's autumn flowering habit.

Nasturtium The botanical name for the common or garden nasturtium is *Tropaeolum majus*, of which there are a number of colourful varieties. The *Tropaeolum* genus itself contains more than 800 species, one of which *T. Peregrinum* is the increasingly well-known Canary creeper.

Oak The oak tree is part of the genus *Quercus*. The Common or English Oak is *Q. robur* – 'robur' was the Roman name for hard wood – of which oak is a prime example. Some species of oak are evergreen, including the Golden oak of Cyprus *Q. alnifolia*.

Olive Olives are now often used as ornamental trees in Britain and their botanical name is *Olea europea* – the European olive. The olive tree has been grown as a source of food and oil for more than 5,000 years and there are a number of cultivated varieties.

———

Ornamental onion Ornamental onions are becoming more and more prized as showy perennials, and like their namesakes the edible onions – plus garlic, chives and leeks – they are part of the genus *Allium*. Their wonderful spherical flower heads are now a familiar sight in many gardens, and the slight onion smell also helps keep bugs away. Popular species include the large *A. giganteum* and the slightly more subtle *A. schubertii*.

Pansy This is the common name for a member of the genus *Viola*. The botanical name for the pansy is *Viola x wittrockiana*, the 'x' showing that it is a cross or hybrid between different species of *Viola*. Though usually grown as an annual or biennial, the pansy is in fact a perennial plant.

Peony From the genus *Paeonia*, peonies provide some of the most stunning flowers to be found in any garden. They have been cultivated by the Chinese since at least the fourth century AD and there are now many beautiful cultivars. These include *P. lactiflora* 'Sarah Bernhardt' and *P. lactiflora* 'Shirley Temple'.

Pinks Pinks, like carnations, are part of the genus *Dianthus*, and come originally from the species *D. plumaris*, meaning plumed, which was later crossed with other species. Modern pinks, which are a combination of old-fashioned pinks and carnations, are more vigorous than the older varieties.

Poppy This is the common name for the genus of plants called *Papaver*. The best known species include *P. orientale* (meaning eastern or oriental) and *P. rhoeas* (the well-known field or corn poppy). The Iceland poppy is *P. nudicaule*. However, the beautiful Blue poppy comes from a different genus, *Meconopsis* – one of the most striking is *M. grandis*. Yet another closely related plant bearing the name poppy is the attractive California poppy *Eschscholzia californica*.

Primrose The ever-popular primrose is part of the large genus of plants called *Primula*. Its botanical name is *P. vulgaris* (meaning common). The *Primula* genus includes three different groups familiar to many gardeners, the Auricula, Candelabra and Polyanthus groups – this last one includes the primrose. As it is such a diverse group, a species or variety of *Primula* can be found to suit virtually any type of garden or location.

Privet This shrub, which is often used for hedges, is from the group *Ligustrum*. The common privet is *L. vulgare*. Some privet can make attractive small trees such as *L. lucidum* 'Excelsum Superbum'.

Red-hot poker This is a very descriptive name for plants of the group *Kniphofia*. Another name is Torch lily. One of the best-known species is *K. uvaria*, which has many popular cultivars such as *K. uvaria* 'Candlelight'.

Rose Perhaps still the most popular and most famous plant of all, the rose is the common name for the genus of plants called *Rosa*, itself a member of the Rosaceae family. The Rose is traditionally divided into three main divisions; species roses (ie those found growing in the wild), old garden roses and modern roses.

Rowan The Rowan or Mountain ash tree is a member of the large genus *Sorbus* and its species name is *Sorbus aucuparia*. There are a number of cultivars, including S. *aucuparia* 'Sheerwater Seedling'. There are many other interesting *Sorbus* species, including the Whitebeam, *S. aria*, and the attractive *S. vilmorinii*.

Sage The herb sage is part of the group *Salvia*, which also contains a number of attractive ornamental species. The sage used for cooking is *S. officinalis*. An attractive ornamental species is *S. argentea*, its name referring to the plant's silvery foliage.

Sea holly Despite its name, this plant is no relation to the holly, but is in fact the common name of the genus *Eryngium*. Sea hollies are striking plants, none more so than the aptly-named four-feet tall, *E. giganteum*.

Snowdrop This is the name for the *Galanthus* genus of bulbs. The species *G. nivalis* is the name for the common snowdrop, nivalis meaning 'growing in snow' or 'snowy'. Popular cultivars include *G. nivalis* 'Flore Pleno' and *G. nivalis* 'Pusey Green Tips'.

Stock Garden stocks are known botanically as the genus *Matthiola*. The biennial Brompton stocks have been developed from the species *M. incana*. The popular night-scented stock have been developed from *Matthiola longipetala* subsp. *bicornis*.

Stonecrop This distinctive plant is increasingly well-known by its generic botanical name *Sedum*. A well-known species is *S. spectabile*, and an attractive variety of this is *S. spectabile* 'Brilliant', whose name indicates its charms.

Sunflower The botanical name for the sunflower genus is *Helianthus*, with *heli-* meaning sun and *-anthus* meaning flower. Members of this genus are of course best known for their tall stems and big bright flower heads. There are a number of cultivars of the species *H. annuus* (meaning annual) including *H. annuus* 'Elite Sun'. The Jerusalem artichoke, which is grown for its edible tubers, is also part of the same genus – *H. tuberosus*.

Sweet pea Its Latin name is *Lathyrus odoratus*, odoratus meaning fragrant or sweet-smelling. The sweet pea is by far the most popular of the *Lathyrus* genus, with many cultivars such as *L. odoratus* 'Bijou' and *L. odoratus* 'Lady Diana'. Other similar species of the same genus include: *L. sylvestris* (Everlasting or Perennial pea) and *L. nervosus* (Lord Anson's blue pea).

Sweet William Another member of the *Dianthus* genus (together with pinks and carnations), Sweet William's botanical name is *Dianthus barbatus*. The names means bearded or barbed.

Tulip The genus *Tulipa* is one of the best-known group of plants in the world. They were brought into Europe from Turkey at the end of the sixteenth century and became so popular in seventeenth-century Holland that the trading of tulip bulbs caused a speculation bubble and eventual financial crisis – the so-called Tulipmania. Tulips are divided into 15 divisions, depending on habits and their flower. As well as the many beautiful varieties such as *T.* 'Kingsblood' and *T.* 'Yokohama' there are some fascinating and sometimes overlooked species such as *T. turkestanica* and *T. violacea*.

Wallflower The botanical name for the familiar English wallflower is *Erysimum cheiri*, making it a member of the *Erysimum* genus, a group of plants which has about 200 species. There are a number of cultivars, including *E. cheiri* 'Fire King'. The wallflower is also sometimes referred to botanically as *Cheiranthus cheiri*. *Cheiri* means red-flowered.

Water lily These beautiful plants are botanically known as the genus *Nymphaea*. The white water lily is *N. alba* – alba meaning white. However, water lilies come in a variety of colours, including yellow such as in *N. odorata* 'Sulphurea Grandiflora' As its name suggests, it has a vivid yellow flower and a fragrant smell.

Willow The scientific name for this large group of trees and shrubs is *Salix*. The famous Weeping willow is *S. babylonica*, its name meaning literally that it originates in Babylon. The distinctive Pussy willow is *S. caprea*, its name 'caprea' or 'goat-like' explaining why it is also known as goat willow. Cricket bats are made from the hard wood of the species *S. alba* var. *caerulea*.

Wormwood This less than elegant name is given to plants of the group *Artemesia*. It is thought *Artemesia* may get its name from the Greek goddess Artemis, known to the Romans as Diana, and/or from the ancient Queen of Caria, who was called Artemisia. The species *A. absinthium* has long been used for medicinal purposes and later as an insect repellent, and is known for its bitterness. It is also where we get the name of the drink absinthe, which is made with wormwood.

Yarrow This plant is known botanically as *Achillea*, named after the Greek hero Achilles who supposedly used the plant to treat his soldiers' wounds. One of the best-known varieties is *A. millefolium* 'Fire King' while *A. ptarmica* 'The Pearl' is another favourite. In some circumstances *A. millefolium* is regarded as a lawn weed. *Millefolium* means literally 'thousand-leaved'.